★ Lou Gehrig ★

PHOTO CREDITS
AP/Wide World Photos.

Distributed to Schools and Libraries
in the United States by
ENCYCLOPAEDIA BRITANNICA CORP.
310 S. Michigan Avenue
Chicago, Illinois 60604

Library of Congress Catalog-in-Publication Data
Rambeck, Richard
Lou Gehrig / Richard Rambeck.
p. cm.
Summary: A biography of the New York Yankee first baseman
known as "The Iron Man" because he played in over 2000 consecutive games.
ISBN 1-56766-073-8
1. Gehrig, Lou, 1903-1941–Juvenile literature. 2. Baseball players–
United States–Biography–Juvenile literature. 3. New York
Yankees (Baseball team)–History–Juvenile literature.
[1. Gehrig, Lou, 1903-1941. 2. Baseball players.]
I. Title.
GV865.G4R36 1994   92-40673
796.357'092–dc20   CIP/AC
[B]

Lou Gehrig

by Richard Rambeck

New York Yankee first baseman Wally Pipp was in a batting slump early in the 1925 season. Pipp had batted .295 in 1924 but was now hitting only about .230. Although he had been New York's starting first baseman since 1915, he went to Yankee manager Miller Huggins one day and asked to be taken out of the lineup. Pipp said he had a headache and needed a rest. Huggins gave his first baseman the day off and replaced him with twenty-one-year-old Lou Gehrig. Gehrig, who joined the Yankees two seasons earlier in 1923, had played in fewer than thirty major-league games.

Pipp never started another
game for New York. He couldn't move
the powerful Gehrig out of the lineup.
After the 1925 season, Pipp was traded
to the Cincinnati Reds. Once Gehrig got
into the starting lineup, he started
every game for the Yankees until May 2,
1939. For fourteen seasons, Gehrig was
on the field for the Yankees—every day,
every game. In that time he played
2,130 straight games, a record that still
stands as the longest streak in sports.
In fact, no player even came within 500
games of Gehrig's 2,130-game record
until Baltimore shortstop Cal Ripken
came along.

"The Iron Horse"

People called Gehrig "The Iron Horse" because of his powerful build and his ability to play despite injuries. During his streak, Gehrig broke his fingers seventeen times. One time he was hit in the head by a pitch and suffered a concussion, but even that didn't stop him. He was back in the lineup the next day, and he didn't even bother to take an aspirin for his aching head. Gehrig always played first base, injured or not—except for a couple of times when he moved to the outfield to fill in for some other player who was injured.

Although Gehrig is best known for his long streak of games, he was also one of the finest players in the history of baseball. Nobody, not even his more-famous teammate Babe Ruth, could hit a ball as hard as Gehrig did. Ruth, who batted third, hit more homers. But Gehrig, who hit after the Babe, probably caused more fear for players in the field. "Lou hit the ball like a Mack truck running into a stone wall at 100 miles an hour," said Claire Ruth, Babe's wife. "No opposing infielder liked to see either the Babe or Lou at bat. But they were far more afraid of Lou's bullet-like smashes."

"Lou could probably hit a ball harder in every direction than any man who ever played," said Yankee catcher Bill Dickey. "He could hit hard line drives past an outfielder the way I hit hard line drives past an infielder." Despite his power, Gehrig played in the big shadow cast by the Babe. "I'm not a headline guy, and we might as well face it," Gehrig admitted. "I'm just a guy who's in there every day, the fellow who follows the Babe in the batting order. When Babe's turn at bat is over, whether he strikes out or belts a home run, the fans are still talking about him when I come up."

Gehrig, however, gave the fans plenty to talk about. He hit a total of 493 home runs and led the American League three times. Gehrig topped the league four times in both runs scored and runs batted in. He had an amazing 184 RBIs in 1931, which is still an American League record. Then in 1934, Gehrig won the Triple Crown for being first in the American League that year in batting average (.363), home runs (49), and RBIs (165). (Babe Ruth may have set a lot of records, but he never won a Triple Crown.) Gehrig also played in seven World Series, batting .361 with 10 homers and 35 RBIs.

With Gehrig and Ruth, the Yankees won World Series titles in 1927, 1928, and 1932. Ruth may have been the team's star, but Gehrig was the leader. After Ruth left in 1935, Gehrig helped the Yankees to more World Series wins in 1936, 1937, and 1938. He was the team's captain for most of his career. "Gehrig was the type of ball player who commanded respect, even if you weren't his teammate," said New York center fielder Joe DiMaggio, who joined the team in 1936 and became a superstar soon after. "I not only admired Lou, but I was amazed by him."

Gehrig commanded respect in a low-key way. Born in New York City to strict parents, he grew up to become a shy and quiet person. Gehrig's mother was stern with him, and his father hardly ever laughed. But he loved them both. "He was wonderful to his folks, very devoted to his mother and dad," said New York catcher Benny Bengough. "He was just a good-living kid. You never heard him pop off or get mad or anything. He was shy for a while until he became a star. Everyone liked the guy."

Gehrig had a soft spot in his heart for children. "He used to treat the kids wonderfully," Bengough said. "When he was first with the Yankees, he'd go down after a ball game and play stickball with them in the park near his house." The same person who was soft with children played very hard on the field. One time, Gehrig crashed into St. Louis Browns shortstop Frank O'Rourke to try to break up a double play. The umpires ruled that Gehrig had hit O'Rourke illegally and awarded the double play to the Browns. As O'Rourke left the field, he yelled some angry words at Gehrig.

Apology Accepted

The next day, Gehrig saw O'Rourke warming up for a game and walked toward him. O'Rourke knew he didn't want to tangle with an angry Iron Horse, who weighed forty pounds more than he did. As Gehrig approached him, the St. Louis player almost trembled with fear. "Frank," Gehrig said softly, "I'm sorry I went into you so hard yesterday. I shouldn't have done it." Gehrig then offered to shake hands. "I shook his hand as warmly as if he had been the president and said, 'Forget about those names I called you,'" O'Rourke recalled. "We were firm friends forever after."

Even though the Yankees won the 1938 World Series championship, Gehrig did not have one of his better seasons. He batted only .295, the first time since 1925 that his average had dipped below .300. During the winter of 1939, Gehrig knew it was more than an unlucky streak. He could tell there was something wrong with him. "There were times when he stumbled over curbstones," said Eleanor Gehrig, his wife. "When we went ice skating, Lou started to fall down more than usual, too. He began to drop things, as though he'd lost some of his reflexes." When the 1939 season started, Gehrig just wasn't himself.

Gehrig played the first eight games of the 1939 season, batting only .143 with just 1 RBI. "I knew there was something seriously wrong with him," said New York catcher Bill Dickey. "I didn't know what it was, but I knew it was serious." On May 2, 1939, Gehrig went to New York manager Joe McCarthy, who told the Iron Horse it might be time to quit. "That's the way I feel, too," Gehrig said. "I'm not doing the ball club any good." He went to the Mayo Clinic to find out what was wrong with him. Doctors told him he had a muscle illness, which is now known as Lou Gehrig's disease. They told him he had two to four years to live.

On July 4, 1939, the Yankees honored Gehrig in a special ceremony. Gehrig spoke to the huge crowd: "Fans, for the past two weeks, you have been reading about a bad break I got. Yet today, I consider myself the luckiest man on the face of the earth." Less than two years later, the Iron Horse died at the age of thirty-eight. To honor their hero, the Yankees placed a granite bust of Gehrig in center field of Yankee Stadium. On the bust these words were carved: "Henry Louis Gehrig. A man, a gentleman, and a great ball player whose amazing record of 2,130 consecutive games should stand for all time. The memorial is a tribute from the Yankee players to their beloved captain and former teammate."